The Green Team

Waste and Recycling

Sally Hewitt

W
FRANKLIN WATTS
LONDON•SYDNEY

This edition 2011
First published by
Franklin Watts
338 Euston Road
London NW1 3BH

Franklin Watts Australia
Level 17/207 Kent Street
Sydney NSW 2000
Copyright © Franklin Watts 2008

Editor: Jeremy Smith
Art director: Jonathan Hair
Design: Jason Anscomb
All rights reserved.

A CIP catalogue record for this book
is available from the British Library.

Picture credits: Alamy: 3, 6l, 7, 11b, 14, 16, 17tr, 18, 20,
21, 23t, 25. Cans for Kids: 18br. Fones4Schools: 23b.
Magpie Slick Schools: 13tr. Meadowbank Elementary
Schoo: 15t, Potter Street Elementary School: 9tl.
Shutterstock: 6r, 8, 10, 12, 13tl, 17tr, 19, 22, 24. Yellow
Pages/Woodland Trust: 9t.

Dewey Classification: 941.085

ISBN: 978 1 4451 0599 4

Printed in China

Franklin Watts is a division of Hachette Children's Books,
an Hachette UK company
www.hachette.co.uk

Contents

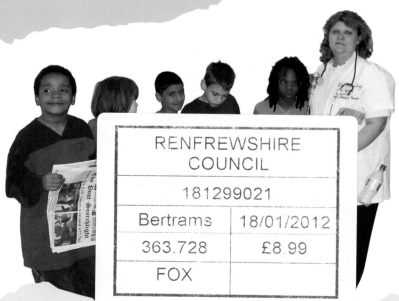

Recycling

There is always an important question to ask before throwing something away; can I reduce the waste I make by reusing or recycling it? If you can't reuse it, then you can save energy and materials and keep it out of landfill by recycling it.

What is recycling?

Recycling means breaking down items such as clothes, computers, tins or bottles, and using the materials and parts to make something new. Recycling uses energy but it uses less energy than making something new from raw materials.

Rubber tyres are shredded and turned into grains of rubber which can be used again and made into rubber goods at this tyre recycling plant.

Look out for this logo before you throw something away. It tells you "this can be recycled".

Different types of materials

Everything we use is made of some kind of material. Raw materials are natural materials, such as rubber, metal and wood, that can be made into things such as tyres, cans or paper. Man-made materials are made from raw materials – for example, plastic is made from oil. Materials can be divided into two groups – non-renewable and renewable.

Non-renewable materials

Some raw materials are not renewable. One day they will run out because we have used them up. Oil is non-renewable. It is drawn up from deep under the earth or sea and used for fuel and to make plastic. Bauxite is also non-renewable. It is used to make aluminium for cooking foil and drinks cans (see pages 18-19).

Renewable materials

Some materials can be renewed because they come from living things. If they are carefully managed they will not run out. Cotton is renewable. It can be harvested and replanted. A sheep's woolly coat will re-grow after it has been shorn. Wood comes from trees and new trees can be planted.

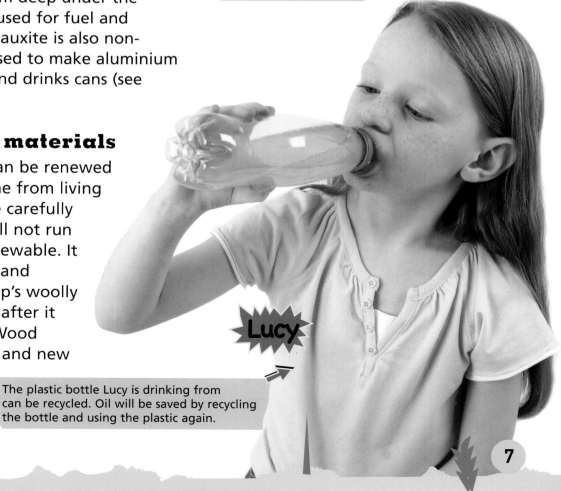

Newspapers are biodegradable. They are printed on paper, which is made from wood. They are recyclable too. They can be broken down and made into clean paper again.

Lucy

The plastic bottle Lucy is drinking from can be recycled. Oil will be saved by recycling the bottle and using the plastic again.

Paper and cardboard

All kinds of different things that we use every day are made of paper or cardboard. We often use them just once, then throw them away. But throwing away paper and cardboard should be the last thing we do when we need to get rid of them.

school book

tissue

newspaper

Which of these things do you use most days? What do you do with them when you have finished with them?

Rubbish!

Paper and cardboard make up the largest part of most household, school and business rubbish. But paper and card don't have to go in the bin.

Paper is recyclable

Even though paper and card are made from wood, which is a natural and renewable material, it makes sense to recycle paper. If you do recycle it, you will save the energy that goes into making paper from wood.

Challenge!

Reduce your rubbish by about 1/3rd.

• Don't put any paper or card in the rubbish bin!

• Take out paperclips, staples, string, glue and paper with a shiny, waterproof coating. What you have left will be "clean" waste paper, which is a good material for making new paper.

The children of Potter Street Elementary School, USA, won the "AF and PA" (American Forest and Paper Association) recycling award for their "We Always Recycle" programme.

We're recycling old Yellow Pages directories here

www.yellow-woods.com

Ian   Lisa   Pip

School children collect Yellow Pages for recycling. They can be turned into animal bedding, cardboard, Jiffy bags, egg boxes and loft insulation.

Case study – Potter Street Elementary, Georgia

Everyone at Potter Street Elementary School, Georgia, in the USA, takes part in its recycling programme. In just 6 months they collected 10,000 lb (4,545kg) of paper and sent it to be recycled. They really have made a difference. The school saves money by not having to pay for as much rubbish to be taken away, and they have also been awarded a grant to help them with their good work.

The Yellow Woods Challenge

The Yellow Woods Challenge is run by Yellow Pages and The Woodland Trust. Yellow Pages make telephone directories in the UK. They give cash prizes to schools for recycling old directories. For every pound of prize money, they give a pound to the The Woodland Trust.

The trust put it towards their "Tree For All" campaign. The aim is to plant 12 million trees over a five-year period – that's one for every child under 16 in the UK.

Action!

Save and recycle paper at school.

• Use both sides of the paper.

• Don't put paper in the recycling bin if you can still use it!

• Put a paper collection box in every classroom.

• Find an organisation such as the American Forest and Paper Association who will work with you.

• Make sure your school buys recycled paper goods.

• Take a cotton handkerchief to school rather than using tissues.

Organic waste

Garden waste and food scraps are "organic" waste, which means waste from living things. Organic waste naturally rots down and can be put back into the soil as compost.

Organic waste can be recycled by turning it into compost.

Challenge!

At home and at school, make sure all your organic waste is collected for recycling or turned into compost.

• Find out if food waste and garden waste can be collected for recycling in your area.

• If not, turn it into compost or ask someone with a garden to turn it into compost for you.

What is organic waste?

Organic waste is all the food waste we throw away. Although all food waste will rot down, it is best to avoid adding cooked meat to compost heaps as this attracts rodents. Food waste makes up a large amount of the rubbish in our bags and bins. Uncooked fruit and vegetable scraps, tea bags and coffee granules, mixed with garden weeds, grass cuttings, pet litter and some paper, make good compost for the garden.

If we don't recycle the organic waste, it all goes to a landfill site, where it biodegrades and makes a liquid that seeps into the soil and water system. This can cause pollution.

Animal waste

People and animals all make organic waste, too, when we go to the toilet. Human waste is called sewage. Animal waste is called manure, and is a natural compost often added to soil to make it more fertile.

Charlize

Charlynn

Chanel

Pupils at Rocklands Primary School look at compost produced by their earthworm factory.

Case study – A wormery in South Africa

At Rocklands Primary, a small school in Mitchell's Plain, South Africa, pupils and staff are developing a vegetable and indigenous garden. Vegetable peelings are brought in from home and added to the school's composting "bath" and earthworm factories. The earthworms produce a rich compost that is perfect for helping garden plants grow quickly.

Case study – Elephant dung

The Maximus Elephant Conservation Trust and Foundation turns elephant dung (manure) into paper (see right). First, the dung is boiled and steamed to kill germs. Then the dung is turned into pulp, which is made into paper.

Action!

Make a wormery.

• You need a big wooden or plastic box with a lid and about 100 worms. You can buy them from fishing tackle shops or collect them yourself.

• To make the bedding, line the bottom of the box with torn up newspaper, compost and leaf mould and sprinkle it with water.

• Add organic waste and crushed egg shells. Cover with bedding and put in the worms.

• Keep the lid on and your compost will be ready in about three months.

• When you want to harvest your compost shine a torch onto the wormery. This makes the worms wriggle down to the bottom.

• Take out the compost and use it in pots, tubs and garden plots to make your school environment a better, more beautiful place rich in wildlife.

Paper pulp made from elephant dung is spread out to dry. After this, it will be ready to use!

Cooking oil

The cooking oil we use for frying chips, stir-frying and making salad dressing all comes from plants. It is made by pressing seeds and nuts to take out their oil.

Maize (corn) is grown as a food and to produce vegetable oil from its seeds.

Biofuel

Oil for cooking comes from many different types of crops. This oil can also be made into a kind of fuel called biofuel. Biofuel means fuel made from plants. It is renewable because it comes from crops that can be grown again, so it will not run out.

Greenhouse gas

Burning biofuels releases a greenhouse gas called carbon dioxide into the air. But the plants that biofuels are made from take in carbon dioxide as they grow. This helps to balance the amount of carbon dioxide in the air.

A growing desire for biofuel means that more and more forests are being cleared to grow biofuel crops.

This is the logo of the Slick Schools scheme in Brighton, which collects used cooking oil from schools and turns it into biofuel.

Biofuel problems

Crops for biofuel can cause problems. If farmers grow biofuel crops instead of food, people may go hungry. Sometimes forests are cleared to grow them. More energy can be used to make biofuels than the energy they actually supply.

Don't throw it away!

When you pour away used cooking oil, it can block up drains and contaminate the water system. You don't have to throw it away. It can be recycled and turned into biofuel.

Case study – Recycling cooking oil

Seven Eco-Schools in Brighton, Sussex, have joined a scheme called Slick Schools. They collect cooking oil for recycling into biofuel. Used cooking oil from the school kitchen and from pupils' homes is collected and stored in a lockable slick bin. Twice a term, the bins are opened for other people, restaurants and take-aways to bring along their used cooking oil.

 ## Action!

Collect cooking oil at home and at school for recycling.

- Oil must be vegetable oil for cooking, not any other kind of oil.
- Vegetable oil mixed with animal fat or water is not suitable.
- Bits of food don't matter. They will be sieved out.

Challenge!

Find out if there is a scheme or company like Slick Schools near you that will collect used cooking oil and recycle it into biofuel. If so, find out if your school is willing to get involved.

Textiles

Clothes, shoes, blankets and duvets are all made of different kinds of textiles. When you have finished with them, they can be cleaned, mended and reused if they are in good enough condition. If not, textiles can be recycled. They don't have to be thrown away.

What do you do with your clothes when you have grown out of them or when they get torn or stained? Many people shop for clothes in charity shops because the clothes are still in good condition and are sold at a low price.

What happens to textiles sent for recycling?

If you send your textiles to a charity, first they will be sorted. Things in good condition are sent all over the world to people who can make good use of them. Textiles that can't be reused are recycled. Woollen clothes are made into yarn to make fabric. Silk and cotton are made into wiping cloths. Other clothes are shredded and made into "flocking", which is used for padding and lining things such as roofs and furniture.

Challenge!

Don't leave unused clothes, shoes, belts, bags and bedding lying around the house.

Sort them into piles:
- things you can use again
- things that someone else can use
- things that can be cleaned, mended and used again
- things to be recycled.

Now make sure everything is reused or recycled!

Meadowbrook Elementary School in Chicago, USA collected the most textiles and won the cash prize for their school.

Design clothes that are good for the planet.

- Have fun and use your imagination!
- Think about what the clothes will be made of.
- Will the material last forever or will it be biodegradable?
- Maybe you can eat your clothes when you've finished with them!
- Can the clothes become something else?
- What can the material be recycled into?

Case study – USA Recycling competition

Schools in the Chicago area of the USA joined in a contest to collect the most textiles for recycling. The company U'SAgain provided recycling boxes for the school grounds. Anyone from the area could drop off clothes and shoes for recycling. Each school that took part received $40 (about £20) for every tonne of textiles they collected.

Imagination

Old clothes can be recycled in all kinds of imaginative ways. One company recycles old denim jeans and turns them into shoes and sandals, so you can wear your old jeans on you feet! Unsold jeans from charity shops and warehouses are bought up and turned into shoes and sandals. Using denim that has already been manufactured helps to save energy and look after the planet.

You can recycle natural fibres such as wool, cotton and silk by cutting them into pieces and adding them in small amounts to the compost heap.

Old denim can be turned into a new pair of shoes, like this pair above.

Plastic

The raw material used to make plastic is oil, a fossil fuel that will run out one day. Some plastic is biodegradable – it will break down and become part of the soil or ground again – but most plastic will stay around and pollute the soil, water and air.

Plastic can be recycled but it needs to be sorted first because each kind of plastic is recycled separately.

Some plastic rings for drinks cans are photodegradable.

Look out for a number inside a recycling triangle stamped on plastic items.

It tells you what kind of plastic it is made of and if it can be recycled.

1 – Drinks bottles

2 – Milk and washing up liquid containers

3 – Food trays, cling film, shampoo bottles

4 – Carrier bags

Photodegradable plastic

There is a kind of plastic called photodegradable plastic. This plastic is better for the environment because it breaks down in sunlight. Photodegradable plastic can also be recycled.

Challenge!

Don't throw plastic away!

- Sort and recycle plastic by numbers.
- Numbers 1 and 2 can be recycled more easily (see page 16).
- Remove the plastic top then wash and squash.
- Supermarkets often have a recycling bin for plastic bags.
- Reduce your use of plastic items that can't be recycled.

Plastic and landfill sites

If we throw plastic away, it eventually ends up in a landfill site. Photodegrable plastic will eventually rot down, and a new generation of plastic bags with corn starch or vegetable oil added to them will also biodegrade. But many plastic bags will never rot down, and we should try and reuse these.

Action!

Have a plastic bag collection at school.

- Get everyone to bring their plastic bags from home.
- Share them out.
- How many times and how many different ways can you reuse each bag?
- Use your imagination and share your ideas.
- When the bags are worn out, take them back to the store for recycling.
- Take cloth bags shopping when all the plastic bags are used up.

This steamroller is making a new road surface from ash produced by burning plastic.

Waste to energy

Plastic is made from oil, a fossil fuel. So if plastic is burnt, it can be turned back into energy to make electricity! The smoke has to be cleaned before it can be released into the air. When the ash has been checked for pollution, it can be used to build roads and to make other building materials.

Metal

Metal is a raw material mined from rocks and earth. It is non-renewable. Valuable metals are hardly every thrown away, but millions of food and drinks cans made of steel and aluminium are thrown away all over the world every day.

Millions of drinks cans are produced every year. They take a lot of energy to make, so don't just throw them away.

Aluminium and steel

Drinks cans are made from aluminium and food cans are made from steel. If they are thrown away they become "scrap metal". Aluminium and steel scrap metal is valuable and can be recycled so it doesn't make sense to throw it away. Steel can be picked out of rubbish by giant magnets and recycled but aluminium is not magnetic, and needs to be put in the recycling bin.

In Cyprus, one recycling scheme has collected more than 16 million cans. Their value has paid for £125,000 worth of equipment for the Makarios Hospital in Nicosia.

Challenge!

Recycle cans!

- If you buy a can of drink when you are out and there is nowhere to recycle it, take it home and put it in your recycling bin.
- Squash aluminium drinks cans so they take up less space.
- Rinse steel food cans such as cans of baked beans and soup.

Case study – Cans For Kids

Cans For Kids is a registered charity, formed in 1990 to organise the collection and recycling of aluminium cans in Cyprus. The charity uses the proceeds from recycling to purchase medical equipment for the children's wards at Cypriot hospitals. Cans For Kids raises awareness of the benefits of recycling by visiting schools to give talks and show the Cans For Kids video explaining why we should recycle aluminium.

Aluminuium oxide being smelted into metal bars.

Making a new aluminum can

It takes a lot to create a new drinks can. A raw material called "bauxite" is mined, then taken to a mill and turned into aluminium oxide. This is then shipped across the water for thousands of kilometres to an hydro-electric plant. Here it is smelted down into metal bars. The bars are then shipped to another country where they are rolled into sheets before finally arriving in the country they will be used in. Once the sheets get there, they are formed into cans, sent to a bottler to be filled with drink, and then delivered to the shops.

In the UK, most of the bauxite in a can comes all the way from Australia and is shipped to hydro-electric plants in Scandinavia. In the United States, bauxite is mined in Jamaica and South America, and processed in North America.

Recycling a can

Cans can usually be recycled without taking such a long journey. Cans are taken from the recycling centre to a scrap processing company where they are crushed into "briquettes". These are then delivered to the aluminium company where they are stripped of paint, shredded, melted and blended with new aluminium and rolled into sheets. These sheets are then delivered to a can maker, sent off to be filled with drink and then delivered to the shops! This uses far less energy – both in making the aluminium and transporting it.

Action!

Hold a school assembly.

Use these facts to convince pupils and staff to recycle cans.

- One recycled can saves enough energy to run a television for three hours.
- If all cans were recycled it would save huge amounts of landfill space.
- What other facts can you find to support your argument?

19

Glass

Even though glass is made of natural raw materials – sand, soda ash and limestone – it is not biodegradable. Once glass has been made, it never breaks down.

Glass items such as these were made thousands of years ago. They can tell us about how people lived in the past.

Recyclable glass

Drinks and sauces come in glass bottles. Jam and honey come in glass jars. When they are empty, we often throw them away. But glass can be recycled over and over again and still make good quality glass. First, the glass is crushed into small pieces. Then it is sent to a glass factory where it is mixed with sand, soda ash and limestone and made into new bottles and jars. Fewer raw materials and less energy are needed to make recycled glass than new glass.

Non-recyclable glass

Not all glass can be recycled. Glass light bulbs, glass cooking pots, mirrors and window panes are not recyclable because other material has been added to the glass they are made of.

 ## Action!

Never throw away recyclable glass again!

Glass buried underground in landfill is there forever.

- Recycle glass at home and at school.
- Put it out for roadside collection.
- Take it to the bottle bank.

Case study – Glass Forever

Glass Forever is a roadshow that visits schools and teaches pupils about recycling glass. The children learn why recycling glass is good for the planet, how it is recycled and what they can do to get involved. The roadshow visited Chetwood Primary School in the UK, and was a great success.

The children got to see glass being recycled into new bottles at a glass factory.

Paula

Andy

Andy and Paula learnt to recycle glass at their local bottle bank.

Viv Hodges, Head Teacher of Chetwood Primary, says: "The children particularly enjoyed the sorting machine. The children are currently doing follow up work on the theme of glass recycling."

Challenge!

Recycle glass and save the planet!

- The energy saved recycling one glass bottle would light a 100w light bulb for four hours!
- Only half the amount of greenhouse gases are made when glass is made from recycled glass than when glass is produced from raw materials.
- Fewer raw materials are used up when glass is recycled.

Children at Chetwood Primary learnt how a glass recycling machine worked.

Mobile phones

Today, we can't imagine life without mobile phones. When a new design comes on the market, many people buy it and get rid of the old one that probably still works perfectly well.

Modern technology lets us chat to friends, listen to music, check the latest news and play computer games wherever we are.

Old mobile phones

What happens to our old mobile phones? They often get pushed to the back of a drawer or left in the bottom of a cupboard. If your old mobile phone is in a drawer, don't leave it there. It is valuable. It can be either used again, mended if it is broken, or recycled.

Throwing away mobiles

Mobile phones contain dangerous chemicals that are harmful to the environment. When a mobile phone is thrown away, it goes to a landfill site where it starts to break down. The poisonous chemicals leak into the soil and then into the water system. The plastic case and metals it is made of are wasted. They could be recycled and used again.

Challenge!

Look all round your house for unused mobile phones.

• Ask, how can they be got rid of in a way that is good for the planet?

22

Valuable materials are recovered and recycled at this mobile phone recycling factory.

Recycling mobile phones

When mobile phones are recycled, the harmful chemicals are disposed of safely. Tiny amounts of precious metals, gold, silver and platinum, are saved and used for jewellery. Copper and nickel are used to make stainless steel products such as saucepans and knives. Plastic is ground down and made into traffic cones.

Being responsible

Unused mobile phones can be sent back to the maker for recycling. You can also collect old mobile phones, win a prize for your school and help to save the planet at the same time! Organisations such as Recycool will collect mobile phones from schools and youth organisations. Prizes are given in return.

 Action!

Dispose of unused mobile phones and equipment responsibly.

• Send them back to the manufacturer for recycling.

• You can save the planet and make some money! Get your school involved in a recycling scheme such as Recycool.

• Schools and youth organisations collect old mobile phones. In return, recycool give them money for every phone they collect.

Visit **www.recycool.org** for inspiration.

Recycool help to save old mobile phones from going into landfill.

Big machines

Millions of people all over the world can't imagine life without a car. They depend on their cars to get to work, to go to school and to visit the shops.

This old car has been dumped, burnt out and left in the middle of the countryside.

Cars pump gases into the atmosphere that cause air pollution and global warming.

What happens to old cars?

When cars are about 14 years old, they usually reach the end of their lives and they are either scrapped or dumped.

Scrapped!

When cars are scrapped, three-quarters of their weight is reused and recycled.
- Aluminium and steel are recovered and recycled.
- Rubber tyres are shredded and recycled.
- The working parts are resold and used again.
- Fuel, oil and anti-freeze are all recovered and recycled.

Challenge!

If your family car is ready for the scrap heap:

- Make sure it is taken to a scrapyard where as much as possible is recycled.
- Find out where the parts can be recycled and disposed of safely.

Dumped!

When cars are dumped, everything goes to waste and the environment is damaged.

- All the valuable materials they are made from are wasted.
- The working parts become useless.
- Fuel, oil and anti-freeze cause pollution.

White goods

Fridges, freezers, cookers, washing machines, dryers and dishwashers are called white goods because they are

Old white goods in working order can be used again by someone else. Others need to be correctly recycled.

➡ Action!

If your family or school needs to get rid of a fridge or another big machine, make sure it is disposed of responsibly.

- Make sure it is clean and empty.
- If it is reusable, find who will collect it for reuse.
- If it is going to be recycled, check that harmful substances will be disposed of safely and that metal and plastic will be shredded and recycled.

usually white. They are big machines that can cause pollution if they are not disposed of and recycled properly.

CFCs and the ozone layer

Old fridges and freezers contain CFCs – harmful substances that can damage the ozone layer. The ozone layer in the Earth's atmosphere protects us from the sun's harmful rays. If it is badly damaged, life on Earth is threatened. Now CFCs are banned but other less harmful gases still should be disposed of safely.

Hole in the ozone layer

This photo taken from space shows the hole in the ozone layer. Scientists hope the ozone layer will repair itself in 50-60 years.

A recycling party

A recycling party is a great way of putting all you have learnt about recycling into practice. You can have fun with your friends and make sure you don't harm the planet at the same time.

Dress up in clothes made out of recyclable materials with a recycling theme, like this party held at a school.

Recycling fancy dress

You could ask your guests to come dressed up in costumes with a recycling theme that encourages everyone to recycle! The costumes should all be made from things around the house. Don't buy anything new to make them.

This costume and sign were made from things found around the house.

Throw a party and make very little or no waste!

- Buy or make recycled paper invitations and party bags.
- Make the party food at home.
- Bake your own cake, make your own sandwiches, serve raw vegetable sticks and fresh fruit chunks.
- Fill the party bags with home-made gifts or gifts made from recycled material.
- Compost or recycle any waste.

Bags of rubbish

At the end of a party, big black bags are often filled with rubbish and thrown away. But everything made of paper and card can be rinsed and recycled several times. Kitchen foil to keep the food fresh can be washed and used again or recycled. If you use china or plastic plates and mugs, metal forks and spoons and cloth tablecloths and napkins, they can all be washed and used again.

This recycled robot costume was made from cardboard boxes, cardboard rolls and used wrapping paper. It could all be put in the recycling bin after the party!

Action!

Make a recycled robot costume from old boxes.

- Don't buy anything new!
- You need a small cardboard box, a large cardboard box, old wrapping paper and glue.
- Cut out a square for your face in the small box.
- Cut holes for your arms in the sides of the big box and a hole for you head in the top.
- Stick the boxes together and cover them with wrapping paper.
- Use your imagination. You could decorate your robot with things that can be recycled.

After this party, all the paper and card was sent off for recycling.

Glossary

Biodegrade
When something biodegrades, it breaks down naturally and becomes part of the soil, water or air. Vegetable peelings are biodegrade but most plastic is not.

Chemicals
Chemicals are substances we use for all kinds of things, including cleaning, cooking and killing pests. Some chemicals can damage the environment.

Compost
Compost is decayed organic material such as plants, food waste and paper. It can be dug into the soil to make it richer and better for growing things.

Fossil fuel
A fuel that is made from the ancient remains of an animal or plant.

Greenhouse gas
A gas such as carbon dioxide that leads to the warming of the Earth's surface.

Indigenous
Something native to a particular country.

Landfill
A way of getting rid of waste by burying it in the ground.

Ozone layer
A layer high up in the atmosphere that protects Earth from the harmful rays of the sun.

Pollute
To pollute means to harm the natural environment such as air, soil or water. Exhaust fumes from cars pollute the air. Oil spills at sea pollute the water.

Recover
When useful materials or working parts are saved and taken out of things that have been thrown away, we say they have been recovered.

Recycle
To recycle something is to break it down and use the material and working parts to make something new.

Textile
A textile is a cloth or fabric made by weaving or knitting yarn or thread.

Wormery
A wormery uses worms to help break down organic material such as food and plants to make compost.

Weblinks

http://www.woodland-trust.org.uk/yell
The Woodland Trust is the UK's leading woodland conservation charity. It is working with Yell, the publisher of Yellow Pages directories, on the Yellow Woods Challenge, helping children to recycle Yellow Pages directories and win cash prizes for their schools.

http://www.magpie.coop/slick_schools.php
Slick Schools is a scheme to collect waste oil from schools and transform it into environmentally-friendly bio-diesel.

http://www.recycool.org
Recycool is a fun recycling campaign for schools. They work with thousands of schools across the UK and Ireland and help to raise money for participants.

http://www.olliesworld.com
A website for children to learn to reduce, reuse and recycle.

http://www.eco-schools.org.uk
Your school can become part of a group of schools committed to saving the planet and caring for the environment.

Note to parents and teachers:

Every effort has been made by the Publishers to ensure that these websites are suitable for children, that they are of the highest educational value, and that they contain no inappropriate or offensive material. However, because of the nature of the Internet, it is impossible to guarantee that the contents of these sites will not be altered. We strongly advise that Internet access is supervised by a responsible adult.

Index